Animals

Penny King & Clare Roundhill

Crabtree Publishing Company

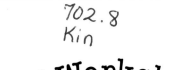

Crabtree Publishing Company

350 Fifth Avenue	360 York Road, R.R.4	73 Lime Walk
Suite 3308	Niagara-on-the-Lake	Headington, Oxford
New York, NY 10118	Ontario L0S 1J0	England 0X3 7AD

Edited by **Bobbie Kalman**
Designed by **Jane Warring**
Illustrations by **Lindy Norton**
Children's pictures by
**Amber Civardi, Camilla Cramsie, Louise Cramsie, Charlotte Downham,
Lara Haworth, Lucinda Howells, Sophie Johns, Lucy MacDonald Watson,
Zoë More O'Ferrall, Gussie Pownall, Thomas Stofer, Ned Wyndham**
Pottery by Chloë Thomson
Picture research by **Sara Elliott**
Photographs by **Peter Millard**

Created by
Thumbprint Books

Copyright © 1996 Thumbprint Books

Cataloging-in-Publication Data
Roundhill, Clare, 1964-
Animals/Clare Roundhill & Penny King
(Artists' workshop)
Includes index.
ISBN 0-86505-851-2 (hc)   ISBN 0-86505-861-X (pbk)
Presents six works of art each of which features an animal, has a different purpose,
and uses a different technique. Includes instructions for creating one's own work.
1. Art-Technique-Juvenile literature. 2. Animals in art-Juvenile literature.
I. King, Penny, 1963- . II. Title. III Series.
N7660.R63 1996   702'.8   LC 95-50852
                                    CIP

First published in 1996 by
A & C Black (Publishers) Limited
35 Bedford Row, London WC1R 4JH

Printed and bound in Singapore

Cover Photograph: **Franz Marc** Blue Horse 1 1911
Franz Marc was a German artist who particularly loved nature and animals. He thought
animals were more beautiful and purer than people. He tried to give the animals life by
painting them in vivid, strong colors and showing their flowing movements.

Contents

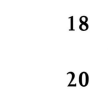

Animals in art

Animals have been shown in art throughout history, ever since prehistoric people first painted them on cave walls. They have been admired, loved and feared for their speed, strength, fierceness and skill.

Muséum d' Histoire Naturelle, Le Havre

Sometimes animals were worshipped as gods or used as symbols of power or good luck. In Ancient Egypt, the cat was thought to be a goddess who guarded people against diseases and evil spirits. At other times, animals were painted or sculpted because of their beauty or because they were much-loved pets.

Before photography, explorers took artists with them on their expeditions so that they could paint the animals they found. These paintings were often realistic and gave people who had never seen a wild animal an idea of how it looked.

Pictures are also a useful way of finding out about all kinds of animals that are now extinct. Cave paintings show what a mammoth looked like. On one expedition, an artist painted this picture to show how a dodo looked.

In this book, there are six works of animal art. Each of them has been created for a different purpose and uses a different technique.

You can learn what gave the artists their ideas and discover how they made the pictures and sculptures. Borrow their ideas, add your own and create stunning works of animal art. The pictures made by children will also help you.

Start by painting your own or a friend's pet or copy an animal from a magazine or photograph. Zoo and wildlife parks are good places to find rare animals for you to paint.

You may want to paint realistic pictures with lots of detail or just sketch an animal in its surroundings. Think about its coloring or the pattern of its coat. Is it furry or smooth? Does the animal have big or small ears?

Prehistoric paintings

Deep in a cave at Lascaux, France, are wonderful wall paintings of cows, horses, bison, stags and even a wooly rhinoceros. These pictures were painted thousands of years ago, but no one knows exactly why. Some people think that the cave was a place of worship.

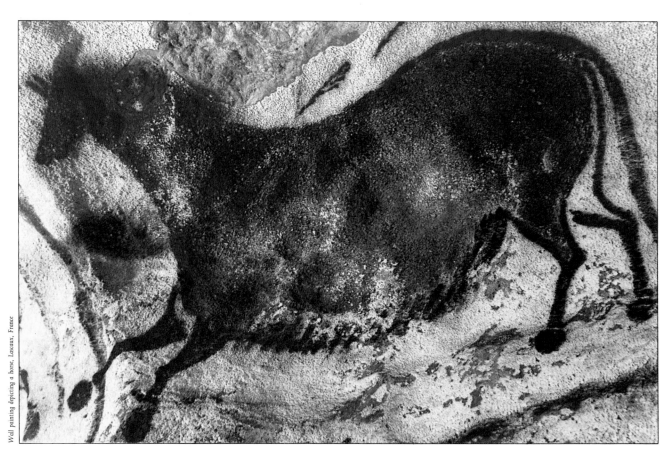

Wall painting depicting a horse, Lascaux, France

Three French boys discovered the paintings by accident over fifty years ago. They were out for a walk when their dog disappeared down a hole in a hillside. One of the boys went to search for him.

The ground beneath the boy gave way and he tumbled into a cave, followed by his friends. They lit matches to see where they were and were amazed to find hundreds of animals painted on the walls.

The prehistoric artists used soil and rocks to make red, black, yellow and white colors. They mixed them with sand or clay, crushed them with stones into powder and added water from the cave.

They painted with their fingers, with brushes of animal hair or used twigs with chewed ends. They worked by the flickering light of tallow (animal fat) lamps.

The artists were very skilled. They never changed or rubbed out any of their marks. They used bumps and cracks in the walls to bring out the shapes of the animals.

Their paintings are full of realistic details about the animals. Ibex (mountain goats) are shown fighting, and bison are shown shedding their winter coats. Some of the horses have detailed markings on their coats.

Stone Age pictures

Imagine you are an artist living in the Stone Age. There are no shops in which to buy paints or paintbrushes. You will have to make them yourself.

You may not be able to grind up rocks to make colors, as prehistoric people did, but there are all kinds of things you can use to make your own natural colors. Plants, fruits, earth and vegetables can all be used to make paint. It is easy to make your own brushes, too.

Prehistoric paintbrushes

Make paintbrushes using feathers or bundles of dried grass tied together. You could also use a twig. Flatten one end with a stone.

Mixing natural colors

Press raspberries, strawberries or blackberries through a strainer to make rich reds. Ask an adult to boil some onion skins in a little water to make orange. Green leaves and grass both make green, and red cabbage and beetroot will give you maroon. Wait until the water has cooled before you use it for painting.

Soil mixed with a little water will make brown. Ground chalk and water will make white.

Cave paintings

Use your natural colors, paintbrushes and fingers to paint bison, cows or deer. You could add some hunters as well. Outline your pictures with charcoal.

Galloping horse

Quickly brush some water all over a piece of paper. Use your natural colors and grass paintbrush to paint a prehistoric horse galloping past a big cave.

The colors will blend together because of the damp paper. When the painting is dry, outline the galloping horse with charcoal.

9

A two-headed snake

This slithery two-headed snake was created by an Aztec craftsman in Mexico about 500 years ago. It is made of wood covered with pieces of precious blue turquoise stones. The mouths and noses are made of red coral, and the teeth are made of shell.

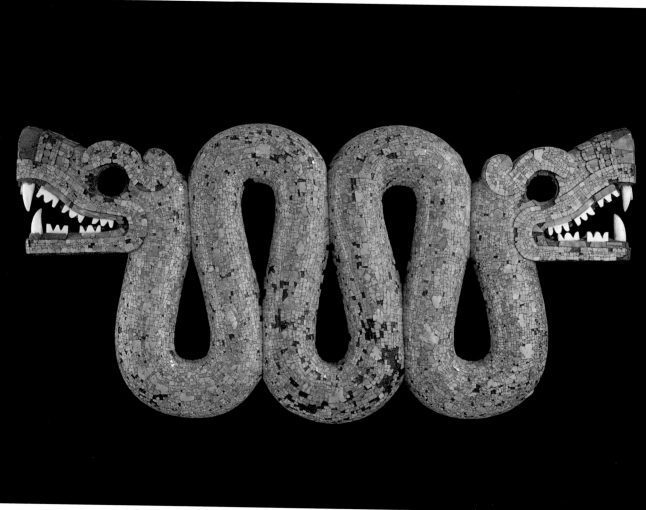

Aztec Turquoise Mosaic double-headed serpent, British Museum, London

The snake represents Tlaloc, the Aztec rain god. The two heads show the coming and going of rain. The Aztecs believed that it was Tlaloc who watered their crops and made them grow.

The Aztecs thought they would starve if they did not keep Tlaloc happy. To pray for rain, they held many festivals throughout the year. At these events, they danced, feasted and made offerings to their gods.

The Aztecs believed that a different god looked after every part of their lives. These gods gave them sun, fire, wind, learning and greatness.

◄ Quetzalcoatl (the plumed serpent) was the god of creation, learning and holiness. This mask of him is made from wood covered with pieces of turquoise.

▶ Huitzilopochtli was the sun god.

◄ Xiuhtectihtli was the god of fire.

▶ Aztec nobles measured their wealth and power by the richness of the things they owned and by the fancy clothes they wore.

Skilled craftsmen made beautiful things to wear of gold, silver and precious stones. These pieces, such as the snake, the mask and jewelry, were worn only on special ceremonial days.

Scaly reptiles

You can make your own precious snake fit for a king or queen. The best materials to use are self-hardening clay and brightly colored oven-baked modeling clay, which can be bought in craft shops. Before you start to mold the clay, soften it in your hands.

Ask an adult to help you bake your creation in the oven to harden it. Follow the directions on the package.

Two-headed snake

Flatten a ball of brightly colored clay (the kind you bake in the oven) into a thin pancake. Cut it into small squares and triangles for the snake's scales. Make lots of sharp white clay teeth and two red clay mouths. Ask an adult to bake the scales, teeth and mouths in the oven until they are hard.

Using self-hardening clay, make a long, slinky snake with two heads. In each head, poke a big hole for the eye. Leave it to harden.

Stick the scales, teeth and mouth firmly onto the snake's slinky clay body with strong glue.

Slithery shell lizard

Color hard-boiled eggs with felt-tipped pens. Peel and break the shells into little pieces.

Use self-hardening clay to make a lizard. Press pieces of colored eggshell all over its body.

To make the eggshells stick firmly, rub water into the clay as you press on the pieces. If you have some sea shells, use them to make a scaly spine down the lizard's back.

Shiny paper turtle

Draw the outline of a turtle on thin shiny paper. Carefully cut it out. Glue the turtle onto colored paper.

Decorate the turtle's body with squares, triangles and circles cut from brightly colored shiny paper.

Make a pattern around the edge of the paper. Add glitter to make your turtle look even more sparkly.

Tropical tiger

How would you like to come face to face with a crouching tiger in the middle of a wild and windy storm? Henri Rousseau, the French artist who painted this picture, became famous for exotic jungle scenes like this.

Henri Rousseau Surprise! 1891. The National Gallery, London

In some of Rosseau's jungle pictures, fierce lions and tigers are shown attacking their prey. Others show mischievous monkeys playing. Rousseau boasted that the ideas for these paintings came from his travels to faraway places.

In fact, Rousseau never left France. He drew the tropical plants at the Botanical Gardens in Paris and copied the tiger from a children's book and from a model. The tiger's eyes look very glassy, just like those of a stuffed animal.

Rousseau did not have any training as a painter. He taught himself to draw and paint by copying famous pictures in the Louvre, a big museum in Paris.

Some people made fun of Rousseau's paintings. They thought his work was too childlike. Several famous artists, however, including Picasso, thought he was a great artist and once gave a banquet in his honor.

Rousseau's style of painting is very distinctive. He used clear outlines and bold colors. Everything in his pictures is very carefully painted. You can see each blade of grass and every leaf on a tree.

Some of the pictures show scenes of everyday life, but the most famous pictures are those with people or animals set in extraordinary or dreamlike settings. This one is called 'The Sleeping Gypsy'.

In the jungle

If Henri Rousseau could paint a tiger in a jungle without having seen a tiger or visited a jungle, so can you. Sketch a tiger from a picture in a book, or look at one in a zoo.

Try to make your jungle as exciting and wild as Rousseau did. Paint a dark, stormy sky, long, thick grass and tall trees bending in the strong wind.

Painted tiger

Before you start painting your picture, mix poster paints with glue and a little flour. They will then become thick and shiny, resembling oil paints.

Start at the top of the paper, as Rousseau did, and paint a stormy sky. Then mix yellow and blue together to make green for the trees and grass. If you want a dark green, add a little more blue. Add more yellow to make a light green.

When the paint is dry, add a fierce tiger leaping through the grass. You may need to paint a few extra blades of grass to hide him.

Wax-resist leopard

With wax crayons, draw a leopard in the middle of a sheet of paper. Color in his white teeth, the black spots on the leopard's body, and the black parts of his eyes.

Use more crayons to draw green leaves, bushes and trees all around him. Have them all bend the same way to make it look windy. Draw the rain with a white crayon and the lightning with a yellow crayon.

Using white and a little black paint, mix a stormy gray color. Add a lot of water and paint the sky. Cover the leopard with thin yellow paint and the jungle with thin green paint. All the parts you drew with wax crayon will shine through the paint.

Torn-tissue zebra

Make a zebra picture using torn strips of tissue paper and scrunched-up tissue balls.

Draw the outline of a zebra on white paper. Tear black tissue paper into thin strips. Glue these onto the zebra's body. Cut out the zebra and glue it onto green paper.

Make a tree trunk with brown tissue balls. Tear green tissue paper into leaf and grass shapes. Glue the bottom part of each leaf onto the tree. Leave the top part to flutter in the breeze. Overlap the grass strips to make them look real.

Saint Francis and the birds

Saint Francis was an Italian saint.
He loved animals and once gave a sermon
to a flock of birds. Stanley Spencer, a
modern artist, painted a picture of this
story. He used Cookham, the English
village where he lived, as the setting.

Stanley Spencer Saint Francis and the Birds 1935, Tate Gallery, London

Spencer painted Saint Francis extra
large, with outstretched arms, to show
that his teachings spread far and wide.
He is looking upwards, as if he were
talking to God. Notice how the
farmyard birds overlap, to show they
are sheltered by Saint Francis.

This picture was entered in an
important exhibition. It was turned
down because people thought
Spencer had made a mistake in it.
Can you see what the so-called
mistake was? (The answer is on
page 32).

Spencer painted many pictures of Bible stories and saints. He modeled the people on his family and friends. He remembered how his father used to go outside in his dressing gown to fetch food for the hens and geese. The dressing gown reminded him of the long clothes that monks wore and gave Spencer the idea for his picture.

The colors in the picture are earthy and natural. Spencer used them to show the link between Saint Francis and nature. He created several shades of green and brown on his palette.

Giotto Saint Francis Preaching to the Birds, San Francesco, Assisi

Compare Spencer's picture of Saint Francis with this wall painting by Giotto, an Italian who lived 700 years ago. It is in the church at Assisi, the village where Saint Francis was born. Giotto was one of the first painters who made people look realistic. When this painting was first created, it seemed very modern and unusual to the people of those times.

Farmyard flocks

These paintings will give you ideas about how to get different shades by mixing colors together. They also show you simple ways of creating a crowd of one type of animal.

Perhaps you'd like to paint a picture of Saint Francis and the birds. You could use one of your parents as a model and your house or village as the background.

Multicolored duck

On a sheet of white paper, draw a simple duck with rows of feathers. Choose two primary colors that go together well, such as blue and red, red and yellow, or yellow and blue.

Put one color into a cup and paint the first feather this color. Add a tiny blob of the second color. Mix it in and paint the second feather this color. Add a little more of the second color to the cup and paint the third feather this shade.

Keep doing this, remembering to add only a tiny bit of the second color to the cup each time, until you have painted every feather in a different shade or color.

A goosey crowd

Draw a fat goose on a piece of thin cardboard and then cut it out. Trace this shape (which is called a template) onto different colored sheets of paper. Cut out the colored geese.

Stick the paper geese onto a piece of black paper so that they overlap one another.

Look at your picture carefully and make a sketch of it. You can also practice drawing crowds of people in the same way.

Saint Mommy or Saint Daddy

For this picture, ask your mom or dad to pose for you in their bathrobe, pretending to be a saint feeding an animal.

Paint a picture of one of them while he or she is in this pose. Use several shades of the same color, just as Stanley Spencer did.

Fante flags

The Fante people of Ghana, West Africa, have been making brightly colored patchwork flags for over six hundred years. The flags are paraded through the streets of towns and villages at festivals and at the funerals of important people.

Asafo flag, Fish Grow Fat for the Benefit of the Crocodile, Peter Adler, London

Fante flags are made of cotton, silk, satin or felt. Sometimes they are embroidered to give them an even more interesting texture and look. There can be as many as 15 different colors on one flag.

The pictures sewn on the flags tell stories of historical events or African proverbs. They show details of the beliefs and traditions of the Fante. This flag's proverb says, 'Fish grow fat for the benefit of the crocodile'.

Long ago, Fante warriors, known as Asafo, formed different groups, called companies. Each company used its own colors and designs for the flags, which nobody else was allowed to copy.

Fante flag designs often include animals, fish, birds, insects, and reptiles, some of which represent power and glory. Elephants and whales symbolize strength. Leopards, eagles and crocodiles are admired for their hunting skills.

The proverb shown on the flag below says, 'Even if you are an able hunter, never dare hunt under the tree of an eagle'.

The biggest Asafo festival is the Akwambo, which means 'path clearing'. It is about friendship and families. The flags are carried in a procession through the town, flown on flagpoles or draped across houses.

Animal flags

Use squares and rectangles of felt or fabric to make your own flags. They will make good decorations for your bedroom or a party.

If you want to make collage flags, you will need fabric glue. If you prefer to make appliqué flags, you will need a needle and thread.

Butterfly flag

Cut out a flag from a large piece of felt and glue a felt border all around it in a contrasting color. Cut out a big, beautiful felt butterfly and two colorful wings. Carefully glue them onto the flag. Add two feelers to the top of the butterfly's head. Decorate the wings with patterns cut out of scraps of brightly colored felt.

Appliqué animals

Draw a large animal, such as a tiger, leopard, dinosaur or lion, on a piece of felt. Cut it out. Sew on felt stripes or spots and a beady eye. Stitch the animal onto a big felt flag, as shown in the pictures. You could also add some trees or leaves on which your animals can munch.

Pretty patterns

Cut out a big felt fish. Sew zigzag patterns all over it, using brightly colored thread for each row. Sew an oval shape for the eye. Stitch the fish onto your flag. You could make a scaly crocodile, a feathery bird or a spiny porcupine in a similar way.

Aboriginal art

The Aborigines are people who have lived in Australia for over fifty thousand years. They have carved and painted pictures on rocks, bark, wood and stone. The pictures are often decorated with elaborate patterns. Susan Wanji Wanji is a modern Aboriginal artist who learned to paint when she was a little girl.

Susan Wanji Wanji Buffalo, Munupi Arts and Crafts Association

When she painted this buffalo, Susan Wanji Wanji combined old Aboriginal ideas with modern materials. Instead of making her own paints, as the Aborigines did, she used a modern paint called gouache.

Susan gets many of her design ideas from the painted body decorations, called Tiwi jilamara, of the Aboriginal Tiwi tribe. They paint their bodies with patterns for important ceremonies.

The Aborigines have their own ideas about how the world began. They believe that everything in the world was made long ago, in a time called the 'Dreamtime'. Many of their works of art tell stories about the 'Dreamtime'.

The Aborigines decorated and painted caves and rock faces with pictures of animals, birds, fish and reptiles. They believed that if they painted these animals, they would always be able to hunt them for food.

Turtles played an important part in their lives: in stories, dreams and as food. Look at this old turtle rock painting compared with Susan Wanji Wanji's bright and colorful modern painting.

Susan Wanji Wanji Green Turtle, Munupi Arts and Crafts Association

Today, a few artists still paint on bark. First it must be dried and flattened. Then the artist covers the bark with a yellow-orange color, called ochre, and draws the animal designs and delicate patterns in white pigment.

Perfect patterns

Kangaroos, wallabies, koalas and birds, such as budgerigars and cockatoos, all live in Australia. Choose the ones you would like to paint or draw and then create your own exciting Aboriginal pictures.

You can use felt-tipped pens, wax crayons or fluorescent paints to cover your pictures with decorations. The brighter and busier they are, the better.

Crazy kangaroo

Draw the outline of a kangaroo in the middle of a square piece of paper. Use a ruler to divide the background into stripes and the kangaroo into different shapes.

Use felt-tipped pens to decorate each background stripe and shape on the kangaroo with a different pattern. If you run out of ideas, look back at some of the colorful and exciting patterns used by Susan Wanji Wanji.

Wax scratch animals

Using fat wax crayons, cover a piece of paper with stripes of color. Press hard so that the colors come out bright. Choose a dark wax crayon and cover the whole piece of paper with a thick layer so that the colored stripes don't show through.

Use something sharp, such as a knitting needle, to scratch a thick outline of a koala or a budgie. Scratch interesting patterns all over the animal and background.

Perching parrot

For this picture, you will need some black construction paper and bright fluorescent paints.

Use white to paint the outline of a big parrot in the middle of the black paper. Using different colored fluorescent paints, decorate either the bird or the background with bright patterns. If you leave the background plain, paint a patterned border around the edge of the paper.

More about the artists

Prehistoric cave painters
(c.17,000 BC   Lascaux, France)
Lascaux Horse

The cave paintings found across south-west France and northern Spain are mostly of animals. Sometimes the artists painted hunters chasing the animals or made hand prints. The paintings are usually deep inside dark caves, where humans never would have lived. For this reason, people think they may have been painted for magical or religious reasons.

Aztec craftsmen
(1400 - 1520   Mexico)

Turquoise Mosaic double-headed serpent
Everyone in Aztec society had a particular place. The ruler was at the top, followed by the nobles, who were governors, judges and generals. The most skilled artisans came just below the nobles. They lived and worked in their own area within the cities and produced precious objects, which only the ruler and nobles were allowed to own. Their skills, often taking years to learn, were handed down from father to son.

Henri Rousseau
(1844 - 1910   French)
Surprise! 1891

Rousseau started his career in the army and then worked at a Paris toll station, (which is why he was later nicknamed 'Le Douanier', French for customs officer). When he retired, he taught himself to paint and started showing his pictures at exhibitions. Several modern artists were inspired by his simple and imaginative way of painting. Picasso, a famous twentieth-century artist, called Rousseau 'the godfather of modern painting'.

Sir Stanley Spencer
(1891 - 1959   English)
Saint Francis and the Birds 1935

Spencer spent most of his life in Cookham, the village where he was born. He thought that Cookham was an 'earthly paradise'. His early paintings were based on people and places in the village, but they all illustrate religious stories. After the First World War, Spencer spent many years painting a war-memorial chapel. The pictures in it show everyday activities in the war hospital where he worked, as well as soldiers washing and eating rather than fighting. During the World War II, Spencer was made an official war artist.

Fante flagmakers
'Fish Grow Fat for the Benefit of the Crocodile (who rules the river)'

Today, a new flag is made when a new captain takes over a company. The captain pays for the flag, but it then belongs to the company. He has a say in its design, which is usually either of an animal, a famous company event or a proverb which shows the company's strength. A flagmaker then designs the pictures in his own style. New flags are approved by the chief of all the companies, as well as by the other local companies.

Susan Wanji Wanji
(Born 1955   Australian Aboriginal)
Buffalo 1993

Susan Wanji Wanji lives in an Aboriginal community on Melville Island in the far north of Australia, where she paints and weaves baskets in an art centre. She spends some of her time hunting, gathering and fishing, which inspires many of the ideas for her paintings.

Other things to do

1 Turn the first letter of your name into a picture of any animal you like or into an animal that begins with the same letter as your name. If you are feeling very ambitious, you might like to turn your whole name into a zoo of animals!

2 Keep a scrapbook about animals. Divide it into three parts: animals you have seen in real life; animals you have seen in books or on TV; extinct and imaginary animals, such as dodos, dinosaurs and unicorns. Practice drawing animals of your own to put into the scrapbook. You can also stick postcards, photographs, cartoons and any other pictures you can find into your album.

3 Model some animals in clay or salt dough. Doing this will help you think about their shapes. Make the body first and then add a head, legs, ears and a tail. Remember to score lines and dampen the parts you are joining together. Press them firmly in place. Paint your models and varnish them when they are dry.

4 Make a passport for your pet or favorite animal. Design an exciting cover for it and write the animal's name on the front. Use a photograph or draw a realistic picture of your animal. Describe the animal's habits, its favorite foods and funny antics. Draw sketches of it in different moods and postures.

Index

Answer to question on page 18: The hands of both Saint Francis and the boy are facing the wrong way. Look at their thumbs!

Acknowledgements
The publishers are grateful to the following institutes and individuals for permission to reproduce the illustrations on the pages mentioned.
Städtische Galerie in Lenbachhaus, Munich / Artothek: cover; Muséum d'Historie Naturelle, Le Havre, (no. 80057): 4; The Ancient Art and Architecture Collection: 6; © The British Museum, London: 10; Reproduced by courtesy of the Trustees, The National Gallery, London: 14; Tate Gallery, London / © Estate of Stanley Spencer 1996 All Rights Reserved DACS: 18; San Francesco, Assisi / The Bridgeman Art Library, London: 19; © Peter Adler from Asafo! African flags of the Fante by Peter Adler and Nicholas Barnard, published by Thames and Hudson, 1992: 22 and 23; Munupi Arts and Crafts Association, Pularumpi, Melville Island, Australia © Susan Wanji Wanji: 26 and 27.